Succeed on the NJ ASK

This Book Includes:

- 3 Practice tests that mirror the NJ ASK
- Answer key and Detailed explanations
- Writing Tasks, Reading Tasks, Language Skills
- Strategies for building speed and accuracy
- Content aligned with the Common Core State Standards

Plus access to Online Workbooks, which include:

- Hundreds of practice questions
- Individualized score reports
- Instant feedback after completion of the workbook
- Self paced learning

Complement Classroom Learning All Year

Using the Lumos Study Program, parents and teachers can reinforce the classroom learning experience for children. It creates a collaborative learning platform for students, teachers and parents.

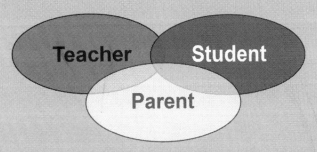

Used in Schools and Public Libraries To Improve Student Achievement

Lumos Learning

NJ ASK Practice Tests and Online Workbooks: Grade 3 Language Arts and Literacy, Fifth Edition

Contributing Editor	- **Anneda Nettleton**
Contributing Editor	- **George Smith**
Contributing Editor	- **Jodi Kaspin**
Contributing Editor	- **Natalie Thau**
Curriculum Director	- **Marisa Adams**
Executive Producer	- **Mukunda Krishnaswamy**
Designer and Illustrator	- **Mirona Jova**

ISBN-10: 1940484006

ISBN-13: 978-1-940484-00-6

Printed in the United States of America

For permissions and additional information contact us

Lumos Information Services, LLC
PO Box 1575, Piscataway, NJ 08855-1575
http://www.LumosLearning.com

Email: support@lumoslearning.com
Tel: (732) 384-0146
Fax: (866) 283-6471

Lumos Learning

Table of Contents

Introduction

The New Jersey Assessment of Skills and Knowledge (NJ ASK) is a comprehensive standards-based assessment administered in the New Jersey schools every year. Student success on this test has significant benefits to all stake holders – students, parents, teachers, and school administration. Success on this test requires students demonstrate good test taking skills and competency in all key areas covered in the Common Core State Standards.

How can students succeed on the NJ ASK through this Lumos Study Program?
At Lumos Learning, we believe that year-long learning and adequate practice before the actual test are the keys to student success on the NJ ASK. We have designed the Lumos NJ ASK Study Program to help students get plenty of realistic practice before the test and to promote year-long collaborative learning.

Inside this book, you will find **three full-length practice tests** that are similar to the NJ ASK. Completing these tests will help students master the different areas that are included in the New Common Core State Standards and practice test taking skills. The results will help the students and educators get insights into students' strengths and weaknesses in particular content areas. These insights could be used to help students strengthen their skills in difficult topics and to improve speed and accuracy while taking the test.

This is a Lumos **tedBook™**! It connects you to **Online Workbooks** and additional resources using a number of devices including android phones, iPhones, tablets and personal computers. The Lumos NJ ASK Online Workbooks are designed to promote year-long learning. It is a simple program students can securely access using a computer with internet access. It consists of hundreds of grade appropriate questions based on the new Common Core State Standards. Students will get instant feedback and can review their answers anytime. Each student's answers and progress can be reviewed by parents and educators to reinforce the learning experience.

LumosLearning.com

How to use this book effectively

The Lumos Program is a flexible learning tool. It can be adapted to suit a student's skill level and the time available to practice before standardized tests. Here are some tips to help you use this book and the online workbooks effectively:

Students
- You can use the "Diagnostic Test" to understand your mastery of different topics and test taking skills.
- Use the "Related Lumos StepUp Online Workbook" in the Answer Key section to identify the topic that is related to each question.
- Use the Online workbooks to practice your areas of difficulty and complement classroom learning.
- Download the Lumos StepUp app using the instructions provided to have anywhere access to online resources.
- Have open-ended questions evaluated by a teacher or parent keeping in mind the scoring rubrics.
- Take the "Practice Tests" as you get close to the NJ ASK test date.
- Complete the test in a quiet place, following the test guidelines. Practice tests provide you an opportunity to improve your test taking skills and to review topics included in the NJ ASK test.

Parents, you can:
- Familiarize yourself with the test format and expectations.
- Help your child use Lumos StepUp Online Workbooks by following the instructions in "How to access the Lumos Online Workbooks" section of this chapter.
- Help your student download the Lumos StepUp app using the instructions provided in "How to download the Lumos StepUp App" section of this chapter.
- Review your child's performance in the "Lumos Online Workbooks" periodically. You can do this by simply asking your child to log into the system online and selecting the subject area you wish to review.

Review your child's work in the Practice Tests. To get a sense of how the open-ended questions are graded review scoring rubrics online at
http://www.state.nj.us/education/assessment/es

Teachers
- Please contact **support@lumoslearning.com** to request a **teacher account.** A teacher account will help you create custom assessments and lessons as well as review the online work of your students. Visit **http://www.lumoslearning.com/lal-quill** to learn more.
- Download the Lumos StepUp app using the instructions provided to get convinient access to Common Core State Standards and additional resources.
- If your school has purchased the school edition of this book, please use this book as the Teacher Guide.
- You can use the Lumos online programs along with this book to complement and extend your classroom instruction.

NJ ASK Frequently Asked Questions

What is the NJ ASK?

It is an acronym for the standardized test administered in the New Jersey public schools (New Jersey Assessment of Skills and Knowledge). It is given every year to students in grade 3 through 8. Students in Grade 3 are tested in Mathematics and Language Arts Literacy. NJ ASK scores are reported as scale scores in each content area. The scores range from 100-199 (Partially Proficient), 200-249 (Proficient) and 250-300 (Advanced Proficient).

When is the NJ ASK given?

It is normally administered in the spring. Please obtain the exact dates of your test from your school.

What is the format of the NJ ASK?

The NJ ASK test typically consists of Reading tasks, Writing tasks and Language Skills. In multiple choice questions, students are expected to select the best answer out of four choices. For open-ended questions, students are asked to construct written responses, in their own words. For the writing tasks a writing situation will be given and questions will asked accordingly. The students are expected to write an answer in their own words. Each test section needs to be completed in the allotted time. Test administrators ensure that students adhere to the test guidelines.

What is the duration of the test?

Grade 3 students take the NJ ASK over a four day period. The first two days are devoted to the Language Arts Literacy test and the next two days to the Mathematics test. On each of the test days students spend from 60 to 100 minutes working on the test.

Where can I get additional information about the NJ ASK?

You can obtain a lot of useful information about the test, schedules and performance reports by visiting the New Jersey State Department of Education's website at http://www.state.nj.us/education/assessment/

Where can I get additional information about the Common Core State Standards (CCSS)?

Please visit http://www.corestandards.org/ELA-Literacy

How to access the Lumos Online Workbooks

First Time Access:
Using a computer with internet access, go to
http://www.LumosLearning.com/book

Select the name of your book from the book selection drop-down menu.

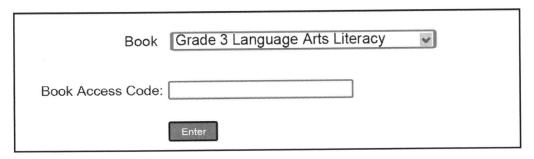

Enter the following access code in the Access Code field and press the Enter button.

Access Code: g3l-932-7778

In the next screen, click on the "New User" button to register your user name and password.

QR Code
for Smart Phone
Or Tablet Users

Subsequent Access:
After you establish your user id and password for subsequent access, simply login with your account information.

What if I buy more than one Lumos Study Program?
Please note that you can use all Online Workbooks with one User ID and Password. If you buy more than one book, you will access them with the same account.
Go back to the http://www.LumosLearning.com/book link and select the second book from the book selection drop-down menu. Enter the access code in the Access Code field provided in the second book. In the next screen simply login using your previously created account.

Lumos StepUp™ Mobile App FAQ

What is the Lumos StepUp App?

It is a FREE application you can download onto your android smart phones, tablets, iPhones, and iPads.

What are the Benefits of the StepUp App?

This mobile application gives convenient access to Common Core State Standards, Practice Test and StepUp Online Workbooks through your smart phone and tablet computers.

Do I Need the StepUp App to Access Online Workbooks?

No, you can access Lumos StepUp Online Workbooks through a personal computer. The StepUp app simply enhances your learning experience and allows you to conveniently access StepUp Online Workbooks and additional resources through your smart phone or tablet.

How can I Download the App?

Visit **http://LumosLearning.com/a/apps** using your smart phone or tablet and follow the instructions to download the app.

QR Code
for Smart Phone
Or Tablet Users

Test Taking Tips

1) **The day before the test**, make sure you get a good night's sleep.

2) **On the day of the test**, be sure to eat a good hearty breakfast! Also, be sure to arrive at school on-time.

3) **During the test:**

Read every question carefully.

While Answering Multiple-Choice questions:

- Do not circle the answer choices. Fill in the bubble corresponding to your answer choice.
- Read **all** of the answer choices, even if think you have found the correct answer.
- Do not spend too much time on any one question. Work steadily through all questions in the section.
- Attempt all of the questions even if you are not sure of some answers.
- If you run into a difficult question, eliminate as many choices as you can and then pick the best one from the remaining choices. Intelligent guessing will help you increase your score.
- Also, mark the question so that if you have extra time, you can return to it after you reach the end of the section. Try to erase the marks after you complete the work.
- Some questions may refer to a graph, chart, or other kind of picture. Carefully review the graphic before answering the question.

While Answering Open-ended questions:

- Open-ended questions typically have multiple parts. Make sure you answer **all** parts clearly.
- Be sure to include explanations for your written responses and show all work.
- Some questions may refer to a graph, chart, or other kind of picture. Carefully review the graphic before answering the question.

Diagnostic Test

Student Name: Start Time:
Test Date: End Time:

Writing Task 1

Here are some reminders for when you are completing this Writing Task:

- Using the situation given below as a guide, write a story in your own words.
- You may take notes, create a web, or do other prewriting work. Then, write your story on a sheet of paper.
- After you complete writing your composition, read whatever you have written. Make sure that your writing is the best it can be.

Jackie and Don woke up early in the morning and found out they did not have school due to extreme weather conditions. It was a snow day! They were very happy. They planned a day filled with fun activities they could do outside.

Write a story about Jackie and Don's fun-filled snow day.

Prewriting Area

Writing Task 1

LumosLearning.com

Reading Task 1

Directions to the Student

Now you will read a story and answer the questions that follow.
Some questions will be multiple-choice; others will be open-ended.

- You may look back at the reading passage as often as you want.
- Read each question carefully and think about the answer. Then completely fill in the circle next to your choice.
- If you do not know the answer to a question, go on to the next question and come back to the skipped question later.

LumosLearning.com

A Dog for Jenny

"You're such a cutie!" said Jenny, a third grader, to her German Shepherd puppy, Madison. She snuggled with her little pal, who seemed very excited from all the love she was getting from her new owner.

"Let's go play catch outside!" Jenny told Madison. Madison, who clearly didn't understand what Jenny said, went along and followed her anyway. Madison's tail was wagging so hard, it nearly bumped into everything she passed! The dog trotted alongside Jenny, and the two looked like they'd never been happier. Jenny continued to pet her as they walked. *She's such a good girl*, she thought.

The two went into the backyard to throw Madison's new toy. They managed to play for an entire two hours! In fact, when Jenny's mom called her inside for dinner, Jenny didn't realize how much time had passed. She kept Madison on the deck while she went to eat her favorite meal: her mother's baked ziti.

Jenny's family just recently adopted Madison from a shelter in New York City. They were looking to share their home with an adorable puppy. They wanted to choose a dog that needed a home, so they made sure they went to a place where dogs were searching for loving homes. As they walked past the charming dogs of every different size, breed, color, and age, they came across a shy, little thing they just couldn't resist. They took her home and she instantly became a member of Jenny's family. Jenny couldn't believe her luck. For her entire life, she'd been so eager to have a dog, and here she was, playing catch with this new little acquaintance.

At one point during dinner, Jenny's mom had asked about the new puppy. Jenny went on and on explaining how much she was enjoying her new pup, how much she loved her new companion, and how terrific Madison was at playing fetch.

"Mom! You'll never believe it! I threw the tennis ball so far, and Madison was still able to catch it!" exclaimed Jenny.

"That's nice, dear. I'm glad you're having fun with her!" said her mom.

"Oh, and one time, I threw the ball so high, and there was Madison, up in the air, trying to catch it!" yelled Jenny excitedly.

Jenny continued to gush about the little dog. She realized that there was just too much to say! At one point, while eating her broccoli, Jenny took a peek to check on Madison.

She looked over to where she left her puppy, and realized that the gate was down on the deck and couldn't see Madison! She ran out immediately to search for her puppy.

"Madison! Madison!" Jenny called as loud as she could as she raced down her street. Several of her neighbors peeked out of the windows to ask what the problem was. Jenny told them what was going on as quickly as she could.

Her next-door neighbors, Jane and Peter, joined her in her search for her new dog. The neighbors, along with Jenny and her parents, went up and down the streets, in and out of backyards, and finally into the woods nearby. They had no luck. Madison was nowhere to be found! Jenny couldn't even think about being without her new friend. The two of them were just perfect together, and as she ran down the street, she got so upset thinking about life without Madison. She couldn't let it happen.

She walked into the nearby pizza place and asked the man at the counter, "Is there any way you saw a dog trotting by?" Unfortunately, he said no. She continued asking people in the restaurant if they'd come across her beloved pup. No one saw a thing.

She ran past a park with some boys

LumosLearning.com

playing basketball outside. She called out, "Anyone see a dog walking by itself?"

"No, sorry!" They called.

They walked around the neighborhood for what felt like hours until they were ready to give up. Jenny was on the verge of tears, but tried to hold back until she knew for sure that they couldn't find Madison. She started walking back to her house feeling terrible when she noticed a tiny head sticking out of the bushes. No, it couldn't be, she thought. But she figured she would peek in just in case.

All of a sudden, there was a sad-looking puppy, looking at her in such a frightened way.

"Oh, my poor little girl! You must've been so scared!" cried Jenny. She was showered with kisses by Madison!

Her parents followed to where they heard their daughter's voice. They rushed over and started petting the cute, tiny animal. "Oh, thank goodness we found her!" Jenny's father said softly. He understood how his daughter felt. When he was younger, he went two days before he found his dog that went loose from his family's home. When they finally found his dog, he had already given up on the possibility that he would find his dog, Muffin. How lucky he felt!

Jenny scooped up her little friend and carried her "bundle of joy" back to their home. Madison looked up at her with love in her eyes. As soon as she reached her house, Jenny made a promise never to let Madison out of her sight. But at the same time, she knew that she'd have a lot of work to do in helping to train this little puppy to listen and stay!

LumosLearning.com

1. What is the theme of this passage?

   Ⓐ A new dog is too much work, because they run away.
   Ⓑ Having a pet can be a lot of work and a lot of fun.
   Ⓒ Lonely dogs make the best pets.
   Ⓓ Jenny has a great family.

2. Choose the answer choice that best describes the setting of this passage.

   Ⓐ The story is set in New York City.
   Ⓑ The story is set in Jenny's neighborhood.
   Ⓒ The story is set in Jenny's house.
   Ⓓ The story is set in a park.

3. Why do you think Jenny didn't realize how much time had passed?

   Ⓐ She wasn't wearing a watch.
   Ⓑ She was enjoying herself.
   Ⓒ Jenny's mom was keeping track of time.
   Ⓓ She was trying to find a new puppy.

4. Which of the following words BEST describes Jenny?

   Ⓐ angry
   Ⓑ loving
   Ⓒ quiet
   Ⓓ hungry

5. What is another word for companion?

   Ⓐ dog
   Ⓑ friend
   Ⓒ animal
   Ⓓ enemy

6. The story states "She was showered with kisses by Madison." What does "showered" mean in the passage?

   Ⓐ to get wet from the rain
   Ⓑ jumped upon by Madison
   Ⓒ licked by Madison
   Ⓓ to take a shower to get clean

7. "He understood how his daughter felt. When he was younger, he went two days before he found his dog that went loose from his family's home."

   Whose point of view are the previous sentences from?

   Ⓐ Jenny's mom
   Ⓑ Jenny's neighbor
   Ⓒ Madison's
   Ⓓ Jenny's father

8. Whose point of view is this story told from?

   Ⓐ Madison's
   Ⓑ Jenny's dad
   Ⓒ a third person narrator
   Ⓓ Jenny's neighbor

9. How did Jenny know that her dog was gone?

   Ⓐ A neighbor called and told her.
   Ⓑ She saw that the gate on the deck was open.
   Ⓒ She saw that the front door was open.
   Ⓓ Her dad saw Madison walking down the street.

LumosLearning.com

Open-Ended Question 1

Here are some reminders for when you are completing this Open-Ended Question:

- Read the passage and the open-ended question and write your answer on a sheet of paper.
- Focus your response on the question asked.
- Answer all parts of the question and explain your answer with specific details.
- Use specific information from the story to answer all the parts of the question.

10. In the passage, "A Dog for Jenny", there are pictures that help to tell the story.

Choose one of the pictures and write about how it adds to the story.

- **Describe the details from the written passage that it illustrates.**
- **Discuss why it is important to the story's message.**
- **Explain how you felt after you found it.**

LumosLearning.com

Reading Task 2

Directions to the Student

Now you will read another passage and answer the questions that follow. Some questions will be multiple-choice; others will be open-ended.

- You may look back at the reading passage as often as you want.
- Read each question carefully and think about the answer and completely fill in the circle next to your choice.
- If you do not know the answer to a question, go on to the next question and come back to the skipped question later.

The Aborigines

Aborigines were the original natives of Australia and lived there thousands of years before any other inhabitants arrived from European and Asian countries. They were rumored to have lived in Australia over 30,000 years. In fact, the word 'Aboriginal' means 'first' or 'earliest known'.

The Aborigines lived simple lives. They lived in small groups of about 500-600 clans and each clan spoke its own language. Although they lived separately in their clans, they had many similarities in beliefs and culture. They built homes out of wood and other natural resources found in their lands. Their diet was rich in meat and vegetables and they often hunted large animals, many of which are extinct today.

Since Australia is its own continent, the Aborigines had very little contact with the rest of the world. They had to create their own tools and crop seeds and they worked hard to adjust to their environment, using their creations to survive and enjoy life. One of the objects best known to Australia was invented and used by the Aborigines. This object, the boomerang was a curved throwing stick made of wood. The Aborigines used boomerangs for hunting and recreation. Hunters used a 'returning' boomerang, which would come back to the thrower, for hunting small creatures such as birds; sometimes they would also use it for play. A 'non-returning' boomerang was also used in hunting as well as warfare. Today, using a boomerang is considered to be great sport. Australian visitors can learn how to use a boomerang from actual Aborigines.

The didgeridoo is a device also invented by the Aborigines. This popular wind instrument is usually made of bamboo and is about five feet long. It creates a low, vibrating sound and is often difficult to learn to play, especially for American tourists. Aborigines play didgeridoos in ceremonies such as weddings, funerals, and circumcisions.

There are now fewer Aborigines in Australia today compared to hundreds of years ago. Europeans began arriving in Australia at the end of the 1700's and brought disease that caused many deaths of the Aborigines. Additionally, many were killed out of fear of because the Europeans' wanted their land. Many Aborigines were forced to assimilate into the white, European society.

Over the past thirty years, the Aborigines today have fought for their rights. They have received equal rights, increased wages, and additional land. They are a people of great art, music, and spirituality. Many of the Aborigines that exist today, which make up approximately 2% of the Australian population, earn a living through selling their artwork. Although they make up a small part of Australian society, Aborigines have made many contributions to Australian culture.

11. **What is the main idea of the passage?**

    Ⓐ **why Australia is important**
    Ⓑ **how to play a didgeridoo**
    Ⓒ **the uses of the boomerang**
    Ⓓ **who the Aborigines of Australia are**

12. **Which statement BEST explains why there are fewer Aborigines in Australia today than in the 1700's?**

    Ⓐ **Many immigrated to America.**
    Ⓑ **Many were killed by diseased brought to Australia by the Europeans.**
    Ⓒ **Many were killed in war.**
    Ⓓ **Many were killed by diseased brought to Australia by Africans.**

13. **If the author of this passage wanted to learn even more about the Aborigines, what resource would be the best source for additional information?**

    Ⓐ **this article**
    Ⓑ **a dictionary entry about the Aborigines**
    Ⓒ **a library book about the Aborigines**
    Ⓓ **a website about Australia**

14. **What do you think the word "inhabitants" means?**

    Ⓐ **A person who lives in a certain area**
    Ⓑ **A hunter**
    Ⓒ **A child who intimidates birds**
    Ⓓ **A person who comes from Europe or Asia**

15. **What was NOT an item made by the Aborigines that was mentioned in the passage?**

    Ⓐ **the boomerang**
    Ⓑ **the spear**
    Ⓒ **the didgeridoo**
    Ⓓ **homes of wood**

    LumosLearning.com

16. According to the above passage how do the Aborigines' today earn their living?

     Ⓐ **by singing**
     Ⓑ **by selling their art work**
     Ⓒ **by cooking**
     Ⓓ **by dancing**

17. According to the above passage, about how many people live in a clan?

     Ⓐ **500 to 600**
     Ⓑ **only a few**
     Ⓒ **5 to 6**
     Ⓓ **a few thousand**

Open-Ended Question 2

Here are some reminders for when you are completing this Open-Ended Question:

- Read the passage "The Aborigines " and the open-ended question and write your answer on a sheet of paper.
- Focus your response on the question asked.
- Answer all parts of the question and explain your answer with specific details.
- Use specific information from the story to answer all the parts of the question.

18. According to the above passage how do the Aborigines' today earn their living?

The passage above discusses the lives of Aborigines in Australia.

- Discuss their lifestyle in your own words.
- Describe the objects that they made.
- Explain how they used them.

LumosLearning.com

Reading Task 3

Directions to the Student

Now you will read a story and answer the questions that follow.
Some questions will be multiple-choice; others will be open-ended.

- You may look back at the reading passage as often as you want.
- Read each question carefully and think about the answer and completely fill in the circle next to your choice.
- If you do not know the answer to a question, go on to the next question and come back to the skipped question later.

MERCURY AND THE WOODMAN
Aesop for Children

A poor woodman was cutting down a tree near the edge of a deep pool in the forest. It was late in the day and the woodman was tired. He had been working since sunrise and the strokes of his axe were not so sure as they had been early that morning. As he began to grow even more tired, thus it happened that the axe slipped and flew out of his hands into the pool.

"Oh no!" the woodman cried. He couldn't believe what had happened. Since it was made of wood, it was the end of the axe.

The woodman was in despair. The axe was all he possessed with which to make a living, and he did not have enough money to buy a new one. As he stood wringing his hands and weeping, the god Mercury suddenly appeared and asked what the trouble was. The woodman told him what had happened to his axe, and straightway the kind god Mercury dived into the pool. When he came up again he held a wonderful golden axe.

"Wow!" said the woodman. He couldn't believe what he was seeing. It was the most incredible axe he had ever seen!

"Is this your axe?" Mercury asked the woodman.

"No," answered the honest woodman, "that is not my axe."

Mercury laid the golden axe on the bank of the river and sprang back into the pool. This time he brought up an axe of silver, but the woodman declared again that it was not his own axe since his axe was just an ordinary one with a wooden handle.

Mercury dived down for the third time, and when he came up again he had the very axe that had been lost.

The poor woodman was very glad that his axe had been found and could not thank the kind god enough. Mercury was greatly pleased with the woodman's honesty.

"I admire your honesty," he said, "and as a reward you may have all three axes, the gold and the silver as well as your own."

The happy woodman returned to his home with his treasures, and soon everybody in the village knew the story of his good fortune. As they heard the story of the honest woodman, there were now several woodmen in the village who believed that they could easily win the same good fortune. They hurried out into the woods and hid their axes in the bushes. They pretended they had lost their axes. Then, they wept and wailed and called on Mercury to help them.

"Oh Mercury!" they cried. "I have lost my axe in the woods and it's nowhere to be found! Please help me. I'm just a poor old woodman!"

And indeed, Mercury did appear, first to this one, then to that. To each one he showed an axe of gold, and each one eagerly claimed it to be the one he had lost. But Mercury did not give them the golden axe. Oh no! He knew what they were up to. Instead he gave each of them a hard whack on the head and sent them home. And when they returned next day to look for their own axes, they were nowhere to be found.

Honesty is the best policy.

19. Which of the following BEST describes the organization of this passage?

Ⓐ It told in sequence using first, second, third, etc.
Ⓑ It is a comparison of two similar things.
Ⓒ It is a story of cause and effect.
Ⓓ It is a contrast of two different things.

20. If the reader of this passage wanted to learn more about making axes, which key words should they enter into a computer search engine?

Ⓐ how to make an axe
Ⓑ wood
Ⓒ the woodman's axe
Ⓓ how to chop down wood

21. What does *possessed* mean as it is mentioned in the above passage?

Ⓐ to own
Ⓑ to be obsessed
Ⓒ to care of
Ⓓ to like

22. Why did the woodman cry, "Oh no"?

Ⓐ the axe's handle was made of wood and would be destroyed
Ⓑ he had cut himself
Ⓒ he accidentally cut his friend
Ⓓ the axe would be lost forever in the pool

Open-Ended Question 2

Here are some reminders for when you are completing this Open-Ended Question:

- Read the passage "Mercury and the Woodman" and the open-ended question and write your answer on a sheet of paper.
- Focus your response on the question asked.
- Answer all parts of the question and explain your answer with specific details.
- Use specific information from the story to answer all the parts of the question.

23. **After reading the above story,**

- **Discuss the moral taught by the story.**
- **Describe in your own words why Mercury was not happy with the other woodman.**
- **Explain why Mercury was so impressed by the poor woodman.**

Language Skills

24. Choose the answer choice that correctly completes the following sentence:

_____ bike has been missing for one week.

Ⓐ Andys
Ⓑ Andy's
Ⓒ Andys'
Ⓓ Andy

25. Read the following titles. Choose the one that is correctly capitalized.

Ⓐ All about birds
Ⓑ Woodmen Of The World
Ⓒ Entertaining Stories for Children
Ⓓ Let's make a birdhouse

26. Read the following sentence. Choose the correctly capitalized answer.
Jill asked her <u>aunt Mona</u> how to bake chocolate chip cookies.

Ⓐ Aunt Mona
Ⓑ aunt mona
Ⓒ Aunt mona
Ⓓ Aunt Mona

27. Choose the word that BEST completes the following sentence:

Amber _____ Alicia will be able to attend the party.

Ⓐ or
Ⓑ but
Ⓒ and
Ⓓ nor

28. Choose the word that is misspelled in the following sentence.
I cannot come to your house this evening beacuse of the severe weather warning.

Ⓐ cannot
Ⓑ beacuse
Ⓒ severe
Ⓓ weather

End Of Diagnostic Test

Diagnostic Test Answers

Sample Answer for Writing Task 1

A 5-point response should include

- Answers to all parts of the question
- Reference to the text in the response
- Personal comparisons

One morning Jackie and Don woke up to find they had a snow day due to extreme weather conditions; the two friends were very excited and very happy. They both knew it would be a fun-filled day. They got out of bed and got dressed, then went downstairs, had their breakfast and both ran outside the door as soon as they were finished.

When they found each other, they planned out what they were going to do the entire day. When they started to get their sleds out of their garage they saw their mothers talking outside in the winter wonderland. They ran over to them and explained their plan for the whole day. First they would go to Sunny Side Hill and find a good place to go sledding. Second they would go to Sunny Side Park and find a very good spot in the snowy lawn to see if they had any of the wonderful sticky powdery snow that would help them make a snow fort and many snow balls. Then they would come back to their houses and make snow angels. Finally they would come inside for some warm hot chocolate and have a warm dinner with a nice movie.

The mothers agreed with their plan and thought that it would be appropriate to have hot chocolate on such a cold day. So the two friends set off on their day full of fun and excitement to Sunny Side Hill. They both were very energetic and climbed the hill faster than they had ever climbed anything. When they got to the top of the hill, they got into their red and blue sleds and pushed hard on the snow. They both yahooed and screamed as their sleds raced down to the bottom of the big hill. The wind in their hair and the snow flying off the sides of the sleds made them happier than ever. It was a wonderful day to be playing outside.

Their next stop was to their houses so they could place their sleds back inside and then they were off to the Sunny Side Park. When they got there, they found a clean spot that was completely vacant so they began to build big long and sturdy snow forts. After both of them had finished the last bit of work on their forts they began to make a supply of snow balls. Then they started to throw the snow balls at each other, glaring at each other's eyes. They threw the balls at each other very fast and they hit them very hard. At the end of this vicious battle, the two of the well built forts had holes all over. Then Jackie suggested that the two head home and make their lovely snow angels. Afterwards the two brushed off all the snow that was covering their jackets and started to walk home.

When the two got home it was getting late so they both decided that they would skip the snow angels and start to make a snowman before all the snow melted. After three hours of hard work, Jackie and Don were finally done. Don added the last carrot nose and then they gave each other a big high five. It was six o clock and their mothers were calling them both inside. Then Don wanted Jackie to come over to his house and have dinner and watch a movie. Jackie's mother agreed to the suggestion and said that Jackie needed to be home by nine o clock.

Don's mother had made hot noodles for them so they ate the delicious food and watched

LumosLearning.com

the movie "Harry Potter and The Order of The Phoenix". They both were big Harry Potter fans.

After seeing half of the movie they had hot chocolate with small marshmallows bobbing up and down in the chocolate milk. The movie ended at eight thirty so the two friends decided to play a quick board game of Chutes and Ladders. The game ended at eight fifty and Jackie decided to go home and sleep. So Don said goodbye to his best friend and went to bed himself thinking about what he was going to do in the snow tomorrow. Soon he was fast asleep.

Related Lumos Online Workbook: Introducing and Closing Topics (CCSS: W.3.1)

Reading Task 1 Answer Key

Question No.	Answer	Related Lumos Online Workbook	CCSS
1	B	Setting the Scene ; Alike and Different	RL.3.9
2	B	The Question Session	RL.3.1
3	B	Tell Me Again... ; Caring Characteres and Life's Lessons	RL.3.2
4	B	Calling All Characters ; A Chain of Events	RL.3.3
5	B	Figurative Language Expressions	RL.3.4
6	C	Figurative Language Expressions	RL.3.4
7	D	Whose Talking Now?	RL.3.6
8	C	Whose Talking Now?	RL.3.6
9	B	Setting the Scene ; Alike and Different	RL.3.9

Sample Answer for Open–Ended Question 1

A 4-point response should include:

- An answer to all parts of the question
- References to the text in response
- Personal comparisons

The last picture in the story shows the love that Jenny and Madison share. The dog is happy to be back with Jenny. Look at his eyes. Also, look at how hard Jenny is squeezing Madison.

Related Lumos Online Workbook: I Can See It! (CCSS: RL.3.7)

Reading Task 2 Answer Key

Question No.	Answer	Related Lumos Online Workbook	CCSS
11	D	The Main Idea Arena	RI.3.2
12	B	The Question Session	RI.3.1
13	C	I Can See It!	RI.3.7
14	A	Educational Expressions	RI.3.4
15	B	Cause and Effect	RI.3.3
16	B	The Main Idea Arena	RI.3.2
17	B	The Main Idea Arena	RI.3.2

Sample answer for Open - Ended Question 2:

A 4-point response should include:

- An answer to all parts of the question
- References to the text in response
- Personal comparisons

The Aborigines lived a simple life. They lived in small groups which had similarities in beliefs and culture but each group spoke its own language. They built their homes from wood and hunted large animals for food. The Aborigines made their own objects that helped them survive.

Boomerangs and Didgeridoos are the best known objects made by Aborigines. A boomerang is a curved throwing stick made of wood and the Didgeridoo is a wind instrument made from bamboo and is about five feet long. The Aborigines used boomerangs for hunting and wars, and use them now as a sport. They used two kinds of boomerangs. One returned to them, and was used for sport. The other boomerang did not return to them and was used only for hunting and in wars. Now people use boomerangs as a sport. The Didgeridoo creates a low vibrating sound and is difficult to play. The Aborigines play these in special ceremonies.

Related Lumos Online Workbook: The Main Idea Arena (CCSS: RI.3.2)

Reading Task 3 Answer Key

Question No.	Answer	Related Lumos Online Workbook	CCSS
19	C	Connect the Dots	RI.3.8
20	A	Special Text Parts	RI.3.5
21	A	Educational Expressions	RI.3.4
22	A	Special Text Parts	RI.3.5

Sample answer for Open - Ended Question 3:

A 4-point response should include:
- Answers to all parts of the question
- Explains the meaning of the figurative phrase
- Personal comparisons

In the story, the poor woodman was honest, so Mercury helped him. When Mercury pulled out the gold and silver axes, the woodman said they were not his. When the axe with the wooden handle was given to him he declared that it was his. Mercury was so impressed with his honesty that he rewarded the woodman with the gold and silver axes.

Having heard this great story, the other woodmen went to the forest and pretended to lose their axes. When Mercury pulled out the gold axe they claimed it was theirs'. Mercury wasn't fooled by their nasty plan. He took away their axes and sent them home without anything.

When you are truthful and honest you will be rewarded but when you are lying you will be punished.

The other woodmen pretended to have lost their axes when they had actually hidden them in the bushes. Mercury was not happy with them because they were greedy and wanted the gold and silver axes for themselves. If they had not lied to Mercury, he would have rewarded them.

The poor woodman could have claimed the gold and silver axes to be his. But he did not do so. Mercury was very impressed by the woodman's honesty because he thought that someone as poor as the woodman could have accepted gold or silver any day.

Related Lumos Online Workbook: Making Words Work (CCSS: L.3.5)

Language Skills Answer Key

Question No.	Answer	Related Lumos Online Workbook	CCSS
24	B	Capitalization Dedication ; Punctuation Education ; Impressive Possessives ; Compelling Spelling ; Syllable Patterns ; What's Your Reference Preference?	L.3.2
25	C	Capitalization Dedication ; Punctuation Education ; Impressive Possessives ; Compelling Spelling ; Syllable Patterns ; What's Your Reference Preference?	L.3.2
26	A	Capitalization Dedication ; Punctuation Education ; Impressive Possessives ; Compelling Spelling ; Syllable Patterns ; What's Your Reference Preference?	L.3.2
27	D	People, Places and Things ; Replace Those Nouns;	L.3.1
28	B	Capitalization Dedication ; Punctuation Education ; Impressive Possessives ; Compelling Spelling ; Syllable Patterns ; What's Your Reference Preference?	L.3.2

LumosLearning.com

Notes

Practice Test - 1

Student Name:

Test Date:

Start Time:

End Time:

Writing Task 1

Here are some reminders for when you are completing this Writing Task:

- Using the situation given below as a guide, write a story in your own words.
- You may take notes, create a web, or do other prewriting work. Then, write your story on a sheet of paper.
- After you complete writing your composition, read whatever you have written. Make sure that your writing is the best it can be.

Most kids like playing some kind of sport. Some kids like baseball, some like basketball and so on. What kind of sport do you like to play?

Write a composition describing the sport you like. Explain why you enjoy playing this sport.

 LumosLearning.com

Prewriting Area

Writing Task 1

   LumosLearning.com

Reading Task 1

Directions to the Student

Now you will read a story and answer the questions that follow.
Some questions will be multiple-choice; others will be open-ended.

- You may look back at the reading passage as often as you want.
- Read each question carefully and think about the answer and completely fill in the circle next to your choice.
- If you do not know the answer to a question, go on to the next question and come back to the skipped question later.

LumosLearning.com

Two Peas in a Pod

Michelle and her best friend Tommy had literally been inseparable since birth. Their mothers, who had been so close since high school, gave birth to them two weeks apart. Their moms traded stories while they were pregnant with their first-borns, and often asked one another for advice when necessary. When Michelle and Tommy were born, they were drawn to one another as infants, always staring at one another from their cribs as toddlers. They played together as soon as they were able to walk. Since they lived in the same town, blocks away from one another, it was an immediate friendship.

As both children turned two, their mothers decided that it was time for them to return to work. Rather than separating these two close friends, they chose to send Michelle and Tommy to the same babysitter. The two children were so tight-knit that they were often told to play with the other children, since they only played with each other. It was so comfortable for them to stick together!

One would think that since these two were such great friends they would have similar personalities, but it did not work that way. Michelle was outgoing; always telling other children and adults what was on her mind. "You are so vivacious, running around with all that energy!" adults would tell her. Since she didn't know what that meant, she asked her mother if it was a good thing, and she was happy to hear it was.

Tommy, on the other hand, was much more subdued. As he got older, he tended to let Michelle speak to others and he would stand back and observe. For this reason, he had the ability to memorize what was taking place. At home, he could explain to his parents who was talking to whom, who was playing together, what the room looked like, and how nice or gloomy it looked outside. But as different as they were, Michelle and Tommy went through elementary school known as "two peas in a pod." They were so close that often people would hear, "Tommy and Michelle!" or "Michelle and Tommy!". The only exception was in the class when Michelle would get into trouble with the teacher for talking.

In fact, there was one time when a teacher pointed out their differences, but not for the better. Michelle was told, "Why can't you follow the rules like your best friend, Tommy?" Tommy crouched down in his chair, embarrassed for himself and for Michelle. He felt awful, like it was his entire fault. It almost caused a lot of trouble for their friendship but luckily, Michelle brushed the statement off, and went right on playing with Tommy after class.

When the two friends were in third grade, they were separated into two different classes. This was the first time they were not together. The two of them were devastated! "How could this

have happened?" they wondered. It was their worst nightmare. Actually, this was a planned situation, since the third grade teachers decided it was time for the two of them to try to "branch out" and make new friends. The teachers didn't do this to hurt the two of them but actually thought it might do the two of them some good.

The first day of school was the toughest, especially for Tommy. He was so used to Michelle being right by his side, talking up a storm, that he felt so lonely entering that classroom at 9:00. He felt like everyone was looking at him as he took his seat and tried to smile at his new teacher.

Michelle was incredibly mad at her teacher, even before she knew her. She walked into the classroom with a mean look on her face, hoping the day would go by quickly so she could see her buddy soon. Michelle barely talked to anyone that day, and for once was extremely quiet. The teacher didn't know what to do with her!

     LumosLearning.com

Luckily, life did get better for the two friends. They gradually got to know their classmates, and formed other friendships besides their own. They even had play dates with other boys and girls from their class, and their mothers grew quite happy with this change. It was so much better for them to know other children their age rather than just stick to themselves.

In fact, it was a truly wonderful thing that they had formed these other friendships because one day, Michelle's mother walked over to Tommy's house to tell her the "horrible" news. Michelle's father was being transferred within his company to another location almost 500 miles away!

Michelle's father was happy with this news. He felt it would be a great change for the family which now consisted of Michelle's parents, Michelle, and her little 2-year-old sister, Alison. He promised the family they would buy a beautiful house, with everything in it that they've always wanted. However, the rest of the family was upset since they had made such wonderful friends over the past few years and were so afraid to make new ones. When Tommy found out, he was devastated. He felt even worse than he had when he and Michelle were in two different classes. Whatever would he do without his best friend in the world?

On the day of the move, Michelle and Tommy, along with their parents, cried and hugged, and vowed to stay in touch...and they did! For five years, the families continued to talk, keep in touch, and even visit one another from time to time. They stayed close friends but were able to make new friends as well. And then came the unexpected day that changed their lives.

Michelle's father was being transferred BACK to their original town! This was so exciting! At this point, Tommy and Michelle were both in the eighth grade and were as different as can be. They were both nervous that the time that had passed and the differences in their personalities that had developed would change their friendship.

     LumosLearning.com

1. What is the main idea in this passage?

    Ⓐ Friends should be there for each other.
    Ⓑ Tommy is too quiet.
    Ⓒ Change can be both good and bad.
    Ⓓ Michelle talks too much.

2. How are Tommy and Michelle most alike?

    Ⓐ They talk a lot.
    Ⓑ They have the same mom.
    Ⓒ They enjoy each other's friendship.
    Ⓓ They live in the same house.

3. How did Tommy and Michelle meet?

    Ⓐ in a play group
    Ⓑ through their mothers
    Ⓒ in school
    Ⓓ from mutual friends

4.What happened to cause Tommy and Michelle to be reunited?

    Ⓐ Tommy's family moved to the same city as Michelle's.
    Ⓑ Michelle's parents got a divorce and her mom moved them back closer to Tommy's family.
    Ⓒ Michelle's family moved back to their hometown.
    Ⓓ Tommy and Michelle ran away so they could be closer together.

5. How many years passed by from the beginning to the end of the story?

    Ⓐ About 13 years
    Ⓑ About 18 years
    Ⓒ About 6 years
    Ⓓ About 20 years

Open-Ended Question 1

Here are some reminders for when you are completing this Open-Ended Question:

- Read the passage and the open-ended question and write your answer on a sheet of paper.
- Focus your response on the question asked.
- Answer all parts of the question and explain your answer with specific details.
- Use specific information from the story to answer all the parts of the question.

6. After reading the passage above,

- Describe how Michelle and Tommy felt when they were separated.
- Explain how you would react if you were separated from your best friend.

 LumosLearning.com

Writing Task 2
Directions to the Student

Read the poem "The Song and Arrow". After you are done, you will do a writing task. The poem may give you ideas for your writing.

The Song and Arrow

I shot an arrow into the air,
It fell to earth, I knew not where;
For, so swiftly it flew, the sight
Could not follow it in its flight.

I breathed a song into the air,
It fell to earth, I knew not where;
For who has sight so keen and strong
That it can follow the flight of song?

Long, long afterward, in an oak
I found the arrow, still unbroke;
And the song, from beginning to end,
I found again in the heart of a friend.

-- H. W. Longfellow
    (1807–1882)

Writing Task 2

Everything that we do, think, or say has consequences. Just as an arrow that is shot in the air falls to the earth and leaves its mark, the actions that we perform or the thoughts that we express leave their mark.

Write a composition about how your own life can connect to this poem.

In your composition, be sure to

- Describe a situation when your action had a consequence.
- Discuss what your action was.
- Explain its consequence.

- You may take notes, create a web, or do other prewriting work. Then, write your composition on the lines provided.
- After you finish writing your composition, carefully read what you have written and make sure that your writing is the best it can be.

Prewriting Area

LumosLearning.com

Writing Task 2

LumosLearning.com

Reading Task 2
Directions to the Student

Now you will read an article and answer the questions that follow.
Some questions will be multiple-choice; others will be open-ended.

- You may look back at the reading passage as often as you want.
- Read each question carefully and think about the answer and completely fill in the circle next to your choice.
- If you do not know the answer to a question, go on to the next question and come back to the skipped question later.

The Emperor Penguins

Antarctica is a place that often fascinates scientists. In fact, scientists are the only people that actually stay in Antarctica. However, the cold continent is the home to different types of animals, including the Emperor Penguin.

The Emperor Penguin lives in colonies on the coast of Antarctica. It is the largest of all penguins, sometimes as tall as 4 feet and weighing as much as 90 pounds! That's about as big as a third or fourth grader! Penguins, unlike most birds on this planet, cannot fly but they do swim extremely well. Just like all penguins, Emperor Penguins have a short neck, large head, a straight body, a tiny tail, and flipper-like wings. They also have webbed-feet that help them swim well.

The Emperor Penguins have adapted well to the harsh climate which can be as low as negative eighty-four (-84 degrees) Fahrenheit! In order to survive in this type of weather, Emperor Penguins have a thick layer of blubber under their skin which is covered with a layer of feathers. The penguins huddle together in large groups to keep warm. They actually trade places with the others to move towards the middle. This way, all penguins have a turn in the central area, which is the warmest.

The Emperor Penguin is one of the only animals in Antarctica to spend the frigid winters on the cold ice. The summer in the Southern Hemisphere, which is where Antarctica is located, corresponds to winter in the United States. They actually breed in the winter rather than in the summertime like most birds. When the Emperor Penguin meets its mate, the female penguin lays just a single egg, and then leaves her mate and the egg! While she is gone, she searches for food in the open water and can travel up to 50 miles during this time. The Emperor Penguins eat different types of fish and squid.

While the female is out looking for food, the male incubates the egg, or keeps it warm, during the winter by balancing it under its stomach and on top of his feet. The male stands with the egg balanced for about 65 days even with freezing temperatures, wind, and snow storms that

     LumosLearning.com

take place around him! He doesn't eat this entire time! Finally, after about two months, the female returns with food for themselves and their new babies. The males take off for their turn finding food, leaving the mom to nurture her new addition.

When the eggs hatch, the newborn Emperor Penguins stay within their mother's pouch so they don't freeze. The baby chicks are called crèches. When they are slightly older, they often group together in order to keep warm.

Throughout their lives, these penguins make sure to work together to try to survive the freezing climate of Antarctica. They are animals that we continue to watch and study because of the way they adapt to their environment.

7. What was the author's purpose for writing this passage?

Ⓐ to write about Antarctica and the freezing temperatures
Ⓑ to show how cold Antarctica can get and why it gets that cold
Ⓒ to write about Emperor Penguins and how they survive the cold weather
Ⓓ to show why no one lives in Antarctica

8. Choose the answer choice that shows how penguins live.

Ⓐ in colonies
Ⓑ with their families
Ⓒ by themselves
Ⓓ with a mate

9. The passage says "Antarctica is a place that often fascinate scientists." What is another word for "fascinates"?

Ⓐ screams
Ⓑ teaches
Ⓒ swims
Ⓓ interests

10. Choose the answer choice that occurs first in the life of an Emperor Penguin.

Ⓐ The male incubates the egg.
Ⓑ The baby penguin is born.
Ⓒ The baby penguins huddle together to keep warm.
Ⓓ The female lays her egg and leaves to find food.

11. **The passage states "The mates take off for their turn finding food, leaving the mom to nurture her new addition." What does "nurture" mean?**

Ⓐ to argue
Ⓑ to care for
Ⓒ to yell at
Ⓓ to call for help

12. **Why do newborn Emperor Penguins stay inside their mother's pouch?**

Ⓐ because they are scared of the other penguins
Ⓑ so they do not freeze
Ⓒ because they do not want scientists looking at them
Ⓓ because they do not know how to walk yet

13. **What allows the penguins to survive in Antarctica's climate?**

Ⓐ working together
Ⓑ migration
Ⓒ staying in the water
Ⓓ their feathers

LumosLearning.com

Open-Ended Question 2

Here are some reminders for when you are completing this Open-Ended Question:

- Read the passage "The Emperor Penguins" and the open-ended question and write your answer on a sheet of paper.
- Focus your response on the question asked.
- Answer all parts of the question and explain your answer with specific details.
- Use specific information from the story to answer all the parts of the question.

14. After reading the above passage,

- **Describe how Emperor Penguins adapt to their surroundings.**
- **Explain how the male penguins help to protect the eggs.**

Reading Task 3
Directions to the Student

Now you will read an article and answer the questions that follow.
Some questions will be multiple-choice; others will be open-ended.

- You may look back at the reading passage as often as you want.
- Read each question carefully and think about the answer and completely fill in the circle next to your choice.
- If you do not know the answer to a question, go on to the next question and come back to the skipped question later.

THE WOLF AND THE HOUSE DOG
Aesop for Children

There was once a wolf that got very little to eat because the dogs of the village were so wide-awake and watchful. He was really nothing but skin and bones, and it made him very downhearted to think of it.

One night this wolf happened to run into a fine, fat housedog who had wandered a little too far from home. He was so starving for food that the wolf would gladly have eaten him then and there, but the housedog looked strong enough to leave his marks should he try it. So the wolf spoke very humbly to the dog, complimenting him on his fine appearance.

"You can be as well-fed as I am if you want to," replied the dog. "Leave the woods; there you live miserably. Why, you have to fight hard for every bite you get. Follow my example and you will get along beautifully."

"What must I do?" asked the wolf.

"Hardly anything," answered the housedog. "Chase people who carry canes, bark at beggars, and fawn over the people of the house. In return you will get tidbits of every kind, chicken bones, choice bits of meat, sugar, cake, and much more besides the kind words and caresses."

LumosLearning.com

The wolf had such a beautiful vision of his coming happiness that he almost wept. But just then he noticed that the hair on the dog's neck was worn and the skin was chafed.

"What is that on your neck?"

"Nothing at all," replied the Dog.

"What? Nothing?"

"Oh, just a trifle!"

"But please tell me."

"Perhaps you see the mark of the collar to which my chain is fastened."

"What! A chain!" cried the wolf. "Don't you go wherever you please?"

"Not always! But what's the difference?" replied the dog.

"All the difference in the world! I don't care a rap for your feasts and I wouldn't take all the tender young lambs in the world at that price." And away ran the wolf to the woods. He was happy with his freedom and he wouldn't give it up for anything.

There is nothing worth as much as liberty.

     LumosLearning.com

15. What is the meaning of the word "Village" in the above passage?

Ⓐ Rural area
Ⓑ Urban area
Ⓒ School
Ⓓ Big city

16. What does "Skin and Bones" mean in the above passage?

Ⓐ beautiful
Ⓑ thin
Ⓒ overwhelmed
Ⓓ excited

17. What did the dog have to give up in exchange for having a lot of food?

Ⓐ his freedom
Ⓑ his kindness
Ⓒ his health
Ⓓ his life

18. What is the theme of the story?

Ⓐ Friendship is important
Ⓑ True friends never leave you
Ⓒ Nothing is more important than freedom
Ⓓ Where there is a will, there is a way

Open-Ended Question 3

Here are some reminders for when you are completing this Open-Ended Question:

- Read the passage "The Wolf and the House Dog" and the open-ended question and write your answer on a sheet of paper.
- Focus your response on the question asked.
- Answer all parts of the question and explain your answer with specific details.
- Use specific information from the story to answer all the parts of the question.

19. After reading the above stories,

- Discuss the moral taught by this story.
- Describe the differences between the life of the wolf and the dog.
- Explain why the wolf would not part with his freedom for food.

Language Skills

20. Choose the phrase that correctly completes the following sentence.

They _____ to my house after school today.

Ⓐ runs
Ⓑ dance
Ⓒ walks
Ⓓ will walk

21. Choose the address that is written entirely correct.

Ⓐ 172 Easy Street
Saint Louis MO 12345

Ⓑ 172 Easy Street,
Saint Louis, MO 12345

Ⓒ 172 Easy Street,
Saint Louis, MO, 12345

Ⓓ 172 Easy Street
Saint Louis, MO 12345

22. What does the underlined phrase in the following sentence most likely mean?

She is <u>taking a step in the right direction</u>.

Ⓐ She was in an accident and forgot how to walk.
Ⓑ She is making poor decisions, that will change her life.
Ⓒ She is making good choices to make a better life for herself.
Ⓓ She is learning how to walk.

23. Choose the word that BEST completes the following sentence.

She is _____ at shooting basketballs than him.

Ⓐ gooder
Ⓑ goodest
Ⓒ better
Ⓓ good

24. Which of the following statements would be BEST for starting a speech in front of the school board about allowing cell phones in school?

Ⓐ Listen up, everyone.
Ⓑ While I understand that not everyone agrees with me...
Ⓒ Why can't you just see it my way?
Ⓓ I will not stand for this.

End Of Practice Test 1

Sample Answer for Writing Task 1

A 5-point response should include:
- Answers to all parts of the question
- References to the text in the response
- Personal comparisons

Many kids play sports. Some like sports that use running instead of hand coordination and some like sports that require you to use your whole body. One of my favorite sports is tennis. Tennis is a great sport for all because it allows us to use the entire body while playing. I also like that it can be played as a team sport or as a one player sport.

The equipment used in tennis is a tennis racquet and tennis balls. The game is played on a tennis court with a net. There are 3 kinds of courts: synthetic or all weather courts, lawn courts and clay courts. As singles, two players compete against each other. As doubles, two teams of two players compete against each other. There is an umpire whose job it is to keep track of the scores and all fouls and other rules that the players in tennis need to follow. Another important set of people are the ball boys and girls. When one of the players loses control of the ball or hits it out, the ball boy or girl runs very fast to get the ball so the game can continue. In tennis there are many rules and options that the player has when he or she thinks that something is unfair for them or the other player.

One game in tennis has 4 points (15, 30, 40 and game). Each set has 6 games. There are also some other points and rules stating the points for tie breakers and so on. One of these points is called a deuce. This is when both players have 40. The next point is known as an advantage. This point is given to whichever player earns the next point. Then will come the final point and whoever wins this will be the winner of the game. If the player with the advantage loses the point then the score will come back to a deuce again. Those are the basic rules and scoring terms in the game of tennis.

Of all the sports, the best sport that I have played would have to be tennis. This is because of all the special rules and point terminology, the strong equipment that they use and the fact that the sport requires you to use the entire part of your body. This sport is one of my favorite sports and will always be.

Related Lumos Online Workbook: Introducing and Closing Topics ; Connecting Ideas (CCSS: W.3.1)

Reading Task 1 Answer Key

Question No.	Answer	Related Lumos Online Workbook	CCSS
1	C	**Tell Me Again... ; Caring Characters and Life's Lessons**	R.L.3.2
2	C	**The Question Session**	**R.L.3.1**
3	B	**The Question Session**	R.L.3.1
4	C	**The Question Session**	**R.L.3.1**
5	A	**Tell Me Again... ; Caring Characters and Life's Lessons**	RL.3.2

LumosLearning.com

Sample Answer for Open – Ended Question 1

A 4-point response should include:

- Answers to all parts of the question
- References to the text in the response
- Personal comparisons

Tommy and Michelle were devastated when they were separated by their 3rd grade teachers. That was the first time they were not together. It was their worst nightmare. Tommy found it very tough on the first day at school. He felt very lonely when entering the classroom. He also felt that everyone was looking at him when he took his seat. Michelle was mad at her teacher even before she saw her. She had a mean look on her face when she entered the classroom and hoped the school day would get over quickly. She was extremely quiet and did not speak with anyone that day.

I would be very unhappy if I were separated from my best friend in school. But I would not be mean to anyone. I would go and talk to the teachers and ask them to put us back together in the same class.

Related Lumos Online Workbook: Calling All Characters ; A Chain of Events

(CCSS: RL.3.3)

Sample Answer for Writing Task 2

A 5-point response should include:

- Answers to all parts of the question
- Reference to the text in the response
- Personal comparisons

When I read this poem, I thought about all the little things that people do which affect others. People can do nice things, like help one another, and it could mean a lot to that person for a long time. People can also do mean things that will hurt someone really bad.

One day, I saw an old lady leaving the store carrying many heavy bags of food. She looked like she needed a lot of help. I asked my mom if I could help her and my mom smiled and said, "Of course." I helped walk her bags to her car and she thanked me a lot. I forgot about it until I got a nice card in the mail. It was a thank you note from the lady I helped at the store. I didn't think that helping her was such a big deal, but it must have meant a lot to her. I felt so glad to have helped another person and now know that everything I do affects other people.

Related Lumos Online Workbook: Make Your Ideas Clearer ; Introducing and Closing Topics ; Connecting Ideas (CCSS: W.3.2)

Reading Task 2 Answer Key

Question No.	Answer	Related Lumos Online Workbook	CCSS
7	C	The Main Idea Arena	RI.3.2
8	A	The Main Idea Arena	RI.3.2
9	D	Educational Expressions	RI.3.4
10	D	Tell Me Again... ; Caring Characters and Life's Lessons	RL.3.2
11	B	Figurative Language Expressions	RL.3.4
12	B	The Main Idea Arena	RI.3.2
13	A	The Main Idea Arena	RI.3.2

Sample Answer for Open - Ended Question 2

A 4-point response should include:

- Answers to all parts of the question
- References to the text in the response
- Personal comparisons

Emperor Penguins have adapted well to the climate and surroundings in Antarctica for many reasons. One very important reason is that their bodies are made to survive in very cold weather. Emperor Penguins have a special layer of skin called blubber that keeps them warm. On top of the blubber is a layer of feathers. By having both of these things on their bodies, Emperor Penguins can survive temperatures that go down to -84 degrees Fahrenheit. The penguins also huddle in groups to keep themselves warm. They trade places among themselves to make sure that every penguin gets a turn to be in the center area which is the warmest.

The male penguin protects the egg while the female is out looking for food. The male keeps the egg warm or incubates it by balancing it under his stomach and on top of his feet. He stands with the egg balanced for about 65 days, even in severe weather, and does not eat during this period.

Related Lumos Online Workbook: The Question Session (CCSS: RI.3.1)

Reading Task 3 Answer Key

Question No.	Answer	Related Lumos Online Workbook	CCSS
15	D	Educational Expressions	RI.3.4
16	B	Educational Expressions	RI.3.4
17	A	The Main Idea Arena	RI.3.2
18	D	Educational Expressions	RI.3.4

Sample Answer for Open - Ended Question 3

A 4-point response should include:

- Answers to all parts of the question
- References to the text in the response
- Personal comparisons

The moral of the story is that freedom is priceless. The dog in this story is rich and has everything in the world that he could have ever wanted, but he can never have his own freedom. However someone that lived on the streets would barely get any food for him or himself but that somebody would have all the freedom in the world. They would just have some trouble getting to where they want to go. The president's daughter has everything in the world and can get to where she would like to go but she would have to have permission and many people would be following her all over the place. Freedom is what every kid in the world would want, or should want.

Some of the differences between the life of the dog and the life of the wolf are: the dog is nice and strong and lives with a rich family but the wolf is very weak and poor.

The dog gets to live inside of a very nice house whereas the wolf has to live in the forest and on the streets.

The dog would be fed everyday but the wolf would get very little or no food every day.

One of the biggest differences that the dog and the wolf have is that the wolf gets to roam the entire city when he wants and he can go where he wants. He doesn't have to ask permission of any one or have someone go with him on his trip. However the dog always has to stay with his master and can only go out of the house when permitted or has to go with his master to the places that he takes the dog.

The wolf would not have given up his freedom for anything because in his mind (in my opinion the right mind) he feels that freedom is priceless. It can't replace anything in the world for him. The dog however thought freedom wasn't that great and food would be more satisfactory than freedom. I feel the dog was a little on the right track but at the same time was completely wrong in his way of thinking. I feel this way because if the dog did not care for freedom or anything like that, he wouldn't be able to have any fun. So in a way the wolf and the dog are both right. The best scenario would be to have both freedom and food.

Related Lumos Online Workbook: The Question Session (CCSS: RI.3.2)

Language Skills Answer Key

Question No.	Answer	Related Lumos Online Workbook	CCSS
20	D	People, Places, and Things ; Replace Those Nouns ; Show Me the Action! ; Tell Me More! ; Make It Make Sense ; Mix Up Those Sentences	L.3.1
21	D	Capitalization Dedication ; Punctuation Education ;	L.3.2
22	C	Making Words Work	L.3.5
23	C	People, Places, and Things ; Replace Those Nouns ; Show Me the Action! ; Tell Me More! ; Make It Make Sense ; Mix Up Those Sentences	L.3.1
24	B	Connect the Word for An Effect	L.3.3

LumosLearning.com

Notes

Practice Test - 2

Student Name: Start Time:

Test Date: End Time:

Writing Task 1

Here are some reminders for when you are completing this Writing Task:

- Using the situation given below as a guide, write a story in your own words.
- You may take notes, create a web, or do other prewriting work. Then, write your story on a sheet of paper.
- After you complete writing your composition, read whatever you have written. Make sure that your writing is the best it can be.

The 3rd grade kids in Cooper's Elementary school will be going to the zoo on a field trip. This is an exciting trip for all the kids. There are various animals in the zoo. There is also a petting place where the kids are allowed to feed and pet some of the animals.

Imagine you are one of the 3rd grade students and write a story about this field trip.

Prewriting Area

Writing Task 1

LumosLearning.com

Reading Task 1
Directions to the Student

Now you will read an article and answer the questions that follow. Some questions will be multiple-choice; others will be open-ended.

- You may look back at the reading passage as often as you want.
- Read each question carefully and think about the answer and completely fill in the circle next to your choice.
- If you do not know the answer to a question, go on to the next question and come back to the skipped question later.

LumosLearning.com

Discreet Hans: A Fairy Tale
by Jacob Grimm and Wilhelm Grimm

Han's mother asked: "Where are you going, Hans?" He told his mother that he was headed to Grethel's.

"Behave well, Hans", his mother said.

"I will take care; good-bye, mother."

"Good-bye, Hans."

Hans came to Grethel. "Good day," said he.

"Good day," replied Grethel, "what treasure do you bring today?"

"I bring nothing. Have you anything to give?" Grethel presented Hans with a needle.

"Good-bye," said he.

"Good-bye, Hans."

Hans took the needle, stuck it in a load of hay, and walked home behind the wagon.

"Good evening, mother," Hans, said to his mother.

"Good evening, Hans. Where have you been?"

"To Grethel's."

"And what have you given her?" she asked.

"Nothing; she has given me something."

"What has Grethel given you?"

"A needle," said Hans.

"And where have you put it?" his mother asked.

"In the load of hay, " replied Hans.

"Then you have behaved stupidly, Hans; you should put needles on your coat-sleeve."

"To behave better, do nothing at all," thought Hans.

"Where are you going, Hans?"

"To Grethel's, mother."

"Behave well, Hans."

"I will take care; good-bye, mother."

"Good-bye, Hans."

Hans came to Grethel. "Good day," said he.

"Good day, Hans. What treasure do you bring?"

"I bring nothing. Have you anything to give?" Grethel gave Hans a knife.

"Good-bye, Grethel."

"Good-bye, Hans."

Hans took the knife, put it in his sleeve, and went home.

"Good evening, mother."

"Good evening, Hans. Where have you been?"

"To Grethel's."

"And what did you take to her?"

"I took nothing; she has given to me."

"And what did she give you?"

"A knife," said Hans.

"And where have you put it?"

"In my sleeve."

"Then you have behaved foolishly again, Hans; you should put knives in your pocket."

"To behave better, do nothing at all," thought Hans.

"Where are you going, Hans?"

"To Grethel's, mother."

"Behave well, Hans."

"I will take care; good-bye, mother."

"Good-bye, Hans."

Hans came to Grethel. "Good day, Grethel."

"Good day, Hans. What treasure do you bring?"

"I bring nothing. Have you anything to give?"

Grethel gave Hans a young goat.

"Good-bye, Grethel."

"Good-bye, Hans."

Hans took the goat, tied its legs, and put it in his pocket. Just as he reached home the goat was not feeling well since it couldn't breathe.

"Good evening, mother."

"Good evening, Hans. Where have you been?"

"To Grethel's."

"And what did you take to her?"

"I took nothing; she gave to me."

"And what did Grethel give you?"

"A goat."

"Where did you put it, Hans?"

"In my pocket."

"There you acted foolishly, Hans; you should have tied the goat with a rope."

"To behave better, do nothing," thought Hans.

     LumosLearning.com

"Where are you going, Hans?"

"To Grethel's, mother."

"Behave well, Hans."

"I'll take care; good-bye, mother."

"Good-bye, Hans."

Hans came to Grethel. "Good day," said he.

"Good day, Hans. What treasure do you bring?"

"I bring nothing. Have you anything to give?" Grethel gave Hans a piece of bacon.

"Good-bye, Grethel."

"Good-bye, Hans."

Hans took the bacon, tied it with a rope, and swung it back and forth, so the dogs came from nearby and ate it up. When he reached home he held the rope in his hand, but there was nothing on it.

"Good evening, mother," said he.

"Good evening, Hans. Where have you been?"

"To Grethel's, mother."

"What did you take there?"

"I took nothing; she gave to me."

"And what did Grethel give you?"

"A piece of bacon," said Hans.

"And where have you put it?"

"I tied it with a rope, swung it about, and the dogs came and ate it up."

"There you acted foolishly, Hans; you should have carried the bacon on your head."

"To behave better, do nothing," thought Hans.

"Where are you going, Hans?"

"To Grethel's, mother."

"Behave well, Hans."

"I'll take care; good-by, mother." "Good-bye, Hans."

Hans came to Grethel. "Good day," said he.

"Good day, Hans. What treasure do you bring?"

"I bring nothing. Have you anything to give?" Grethel gave Hans a calf.

"Good-bye," said Hans.

"Good-bye."

Hans took the calf, set it on his head, and the calf scratched his face.

"Good evening, mother."

"Good evening, Hans. Where have you been?"

"To Grethel's."

"What did you take her?"

"I took nothing; she gave to me."

"And what did Grethel give you?"

"A calf," said Hans.

"And what did you do with it?"

"I set it on my head, and it kicked my face."

"Then you acted stupidly, Hans; you should have led the calf home, and put it in the stall."

"To behave better, do nothing," thought Hans.

"Where are you going, Hans?"

"To Grethel's, mother."

"Behave well, Hans."

"I'll take care; good-bye, mother."

"Good bye, Hans."

Hans came to Grethel. "Good day," said he.

"Good day, Hans. What treasure do you bring?"

"I bring nothing. Have you anything to give?"

Grethel said: "I will go with you, Hans."

     LumosLearning.com

Hans tied a rope round Grethel, led her home, put her in the stall, and made the rope fast; and then he went to his mother.

"Good evening, mother."
"Good evening, Hans. Where have you been?"
"To Grethel's."
"What did you take her?"
"I took nothing."
"What did Grethel give you?"
"She gave nothing; she came with me."
"And where have you left her, then?"
"I tied her with a rope, put her in the stall, and threw in some grass."
"Then you acted stupidly, Hans; you should have looked at her with friendly eyes."
"To behave better, do nothing," thought Hans; and then he went into the stall, and made sheep's eyes at Grethel.
And after that, Grethel became Hans's wife.

1. Why did Hans put the goat in his pocket?

   Ⓐ He thought it could fit in there.
   Ⓑ He was being silly.
   Ⓒ His mom told him he should put knives in his pocket.
   Ⓓ Hans didn't like the goat.

2. In what order did Hans receive the gifts?

   Ⓐ needle, knife, goat, bacon, calf, Grethel
   Ⓑ knife, Grethel, goat, bacon, calf
   Ⓒ calf, goat, bacon, knife, Grethel
   Ⓓ needle, goat, calf, bacon, Grethel

3. What do you think is the message the author is trying to convey in this passage?

   Ⓐ Remember to always tie up your goats before bringing them home.
   Ⓑ You should not put a goat in your pocket.
   Ⓒ Think about what people say before you act.
   Ⓓ Hans is a very silly person who likes to fool around.

4. When do you think this story may have taken place?

   Ⓐ 15 years ago
   Ⓑ 80 years ago
   Ⓒ sometime in the future
   Ⓓ today

5. In what type of community is likely to have the lifestyle described in this story?

   Ⓐ Urban
   Ⓑ Suburban
   Ⓒ Rural
   Ⓓ Metro

6. Which of the following characters was NOT a main character in this passage?

   Ⓐ the goat
   Ⓑ Hans
   Ⓒ Grethel
   Ⓓ Hans' mother

Open-Ended Question 1

Here are some reminders for when you are completing this Open-Ended Question:

- Read the passage "Discreet Hans: A Fairy Tale" and the open-ended question and write your answer on a sheet of paper.
- Focus your response on the question asked.
- Answer all parts of the question and explain your answer with specific details.
- Use specific information from the story to answer all the parts of the question.

7. According to the above story,

- **Describe Hans' character.**
- **Discuss Hans' reaction to his mother's advice.**
- **If you were Hans, explain how you would react to the advice.**

LumosLearning.com

Writing Task 2

Directions to the Student

Here are some reminders for when you are completing this Writing Task:

- Read the poem "The World" given below and complete the writing task on a sheet of paper. The poem may give you ideas for your writing.
- You may take notes, create a web, or do other prewriting work. Then, write your composition on the lines provided.
- After you finish writing your composition, carefully read what you have written and make sure that your writing is the best it can be.

The World

The world is wet," said the little frog;
"What isn't water is mostly bog."
"Oh, not at all!" said the little fly;
"It's full of spiders, and very dry!"
"The world is dark," said the moth polite,
"With ruddy windows and bows of light."
"My poor young friend, you have much to learn:
The world is green," said the swaying fern.
"O listen to me," sang the little lark:
"It's wet and dry, and it's green and dark.
To think that's all, would be very wrong;
It's arched with blue, and it's filled with song."

Writing Task 2

The above poem tells us how different living beings feel about the world around them.

Write a composition about what connections you can make to this poem. In your composition be sure to:

- Discuss what character you agree with.
- Explain why.
- Describe your opinion on the world.

Prewriting Area

Writing Task 2

Reading Task 2
Directions to the Student

Now you will read an article and answer the questions that follow.
Some questions will be multiple-choice; others will be open-ended.

- You may look back at the reading passage as often as you want.
- Read each question carefully and think about the answer and completely fill in the circle next to your choice.
- If you do not know the answer to a question, go on to the next question and come back to the skipped question later.

LumosLearning.com

The Amazon Rainforest

The Amazon Rainforest is full of life, with sounds of all kinds, water rushing and falling, and animals communicating with one another. It's a busy place where animals are looking for food, trying to survive, and looking to expand their families. Within the Amazon Rainforest in South America, exists one such tiny animal that is almost completely camouflaged from the rest of the animals, except for one small body part: bright red eyes!

This animal is known as the Red-Eyed Tree Frog and it lives deep in the tall trees within the Amazon. Although they reside mostly in South America, they can also be found in Central America and parts of Mexico.

Bright colors decorate the body of the adult Red-Eyed Tree frog. The main color is green, but there are also mixtures of yellow, orange, and even blue on its belly. The frog can change its colors based on its feelings or needs; the color often changes from green to reddish-brown. On its toes are suction cups that help the Red-Eyed Tree Frog attach itself to its environment. They give the frog traction to stay put on wet leaves. Their legs are built better for climbing than for swimming and they are almost never on the ground. They keep jumping around at a steady pace from tree to tree.

The physical properties of the Red-Eyed Tree Frog also make them different and help them survive. Unlike most humans, or even other animals, the male frog is actually smaller than the female. Male frogs only reach around two inches in length while the females can grow to be three inches. The Red-Eyed Tree Frog is also a carnivore. Similar to other frogs, the tree frog eats grasshoppers, moths, and other insects. However, it eats smaller frogs too! It is known to eat almost anything that can fit in its mouth.

Many people find it fascinating to know that the red eyes are not just for looks; they help the frogs survive. In fact, the red eyes scare other animals easily and help these frogs escape their predators. With their greenish color skin, they tend to blend in with their surroundings. When they sleep, they are virtually invisible. However, if other animals see them and try to attack, the Red-Eyed Tree Frog will open its wide, red eyes and the predators, which usually consist of snakes, birds, or bats, will scurry away. In many cases, the predators may also be stunned into stillness at the sight of the red eyes, long enough for the frog to escape.

The Red-Eyed Tree frog is a unique animal able to protect itself even though very small. With deadly predators and a dangerous environment surrounding it, the frog relies on camouflage and its bright red eyes to scare off unwanted guests and enemies.

8. What do you think would be the best possible title for this passage?

 Ⓐ The Amazon Rainforest
 Ⓑ Interesting Facts about the Red-Eyed Tree Frog
 Ⓒ How Red-Eyed Tree Frogs Change Color
 Ⓓ South American Animals

9. Based on the passage, where can the Red-Eyed Tree Frog be most commonly found?

 Ⓐ The Amazon Rainforest
 Ⓑ South America
 Ⓒ Africa
 Ⓓ Australia

10. What is the main idea of the passage?

 Ⓐ How a Red-Eyed Tree Frog survives
 Ⓑ The Size of the Red-Eyed Tree Frog
 Ⓒ What the Red-Eyed Tree Frog eats
 Ⓓ Red-Eyed Tree Frog males are larger than females

11. What do you think the word "traction" means?

 Ⓐ carry
 Ⓑ move around
 Ⓒ grip
 Ⓓ slide

12. How does the Red-Eyed Tree Frog completely camouflage itself?

 Ⓐ It turns different colors.
 Ⓑ It tucks in its orange toes.
 Ⓒ It opens its eyes.
 Ⓓ It eats grasshoppers.

13. Which of the following sentences is true about the above passage?

 Ⓐ The above passage is a realistic fiction.
 Ⓑ The above passage is a nonfiction passage.
 Ⓒ The above passage is a fairy tale.
 Ⓓ The above passage is a fiction story.

Open-Ended Question 2

14. **After you read the passage above,**

- **Describe two interesting characteristics of the Red-Eyed Tree Frog.**
- **Explain how it saves itself from predators.**

Reading Task 3
Directions to the Student

Now you will read another passage and answer the questions that follow.
Some questions will be multiple-choice; others will be open-ended.

- You may look back at the reading passage as often as you want.
- Read each question carefully and think about the answer and completely fill in the circle next to your choice.
- If you do not know the answer to a question, go on to the next question and come back to the skipped question later.

The story of Albert Einstein

Without any indication he was destined for something great, Albert Einstein was born on March 14, 1879. In fact, his mother thought Albert was extremely unusual. At the age of two-and-a-half, Einstein still wasn't talking. When he finally did learn to speak, he uttered everything twice.

Einstein did not know what to do with other children and his playmates called him "Brother Boring." Because of that, the youngster played by himself much of the time. He especially loved mechanical toys and looked for them everywhere he went. Looking once at his newborn sister, Maja, he is believed to have said, "Fine, but where are her wheels?" Einstein began learning to play the violin at the age of six because his mother believed it was important. He later became a gifted amateur violinist, maintaining this skill throughout his life.

Unfortunately, that awkwardness extended to school as well. A headmaster at one of his early schools once told his father that Einstein's profession wouldn't matter because, "he'll never be successful at anything." But Einstein was not a bad pupil. He went to high school in Munich, Germany, where his family moved when he was fifteen months old, and earned good grades in almost every subject. He hated the strict school environment though, and often clashed with his teachers. At the age of 15, Einstein felt so stifled there that he left the school for good. He then took the entrance exams for college and although he failed some, his scores for Physics and Math were so good, they let him into the school.

In 1900, at the age of 21, Albert Einstein was a college graduate and was employed. He worked as a teaching assistant and gave private lessons on the violin before finally getting a job as a technical expert in Bern's patent office. While he was supposed to be paying careful attention to other people's inventions, he was secretly developing many ideas of his own.

Einstein in 1900 at the age of 21

Einstein in 1955 as we remember him now

LumosLearning.com

One of his famous papers, published in 1905, was Einstein's special Theory of Relativity. This theory had to do with time and distance not being absolute. His theory explained that two perfectly accurate and synced clocks would not continue to show the same time if they came together again after a journey where one traveled at a faster speed than the other. From this theory followed the world's most famous formula which described the relationships between mass and energy:

$$E = mc^2$$

In 1915, he published his General Theory of Relativity, which provided a new idea of gravity. An eclipse of the sun in 1919 brought proof that his theory was accurate. Einstein had correctly calculated, in advance, the extent to which the light from fixed stars would be deflected through the sun's gravitational field. The newspapers proclaimed his work as a 'scientific revolution.'

Einstein received the Nobel Prize for Physics in 1921. He was showered with honors and invitations from all over the world and applauded by the press.

15. When did his family and friends FIRST start beginning to see what Albert could do?

Ⓐ as a baby
Ⓑ as an infant
Ⓒ in his years at school
Ⓓ after college

16. In the passage it says "At the age of 15, Einstein felt so stifled there that he left the school for good."

What do you think "stifled" means in the passage?

Ⓐ loud
Ⓑ discouraged
Ⓒ cute
Ⓓ smart

17. Which of the following BEST describes Einstein's language as a baby?

Ⓐ He was late speaking, then said everything two times.
Ⓑ He never talked.
Ⓒ He said everything two times from the time he was one year old.
Ⓓ He did not talk to anyone, except his baby sister.

LumosLearning.com

Open-Ended Question 3

Here are some reminders for when you are completing this Open-Ended Question: •Read the passage "The Amazon Rainforest" and the open-ended question and write your answer on a sheet of paper. •Focus your response on the question asked. •Answer all parts of the question and explain your answer with specific details. •Use specific information from the story to answer all the parts of the question.

18. **After reading the above passage,**

   • **Describe Albert Einstein's childhood.**
   • **Do you think he was genius? Explain why.**

LumosLearning.com

Reading Task 4
Directions to the Student

**Now you will read another passage and answer the questions that follow.
Some questions will be multiple-choice; others will be open-ended.**

- You may look back at the reading passage as often as you want.
- Read each question carefully and think about the answer and completely fill in the circle next to your choice.
- If you do not know the answer to a question, go on to the next question and come back to the skipped question later.

The Tale of Peter Rabbit
By Beatrix Potter

Once upon a time there were four little Rabbits, and their names were: Flopsy, Mopsy, Cottontail, and Peter. They lived with their Mother in a sandbank, underneath the root of a very big fir-tree.

"Now, my dears," said old Mrs. Rabbit one morning. "You may go into the fields or down the lane, but don't go into Mr. McGregor's garden: your Father had an accident there; he was put in a pie by Mrs. McGregor. Now run along, and don't get into mischief. I am going out." Then old Mrs. Rabbit took a basket and her umbrella and went through the wood to the baker's. She bought a loaf of brown bread and five currant buns.

Flopsy, Mopsy, and Cottontail, who were good little bunnies, went down the lane to gather blackberries. But Peter, who was very naughty, ran straight away to Mr. McGregor's garden and squeezed under the gate! First he ate some lettuces and some French beans, and then he ate some radishes; and then, feeling rather sick, he went to look for some parsley. But round the end of a cucumber frame, whom should he meet but Mr. McGregor!

Mr. McGregor was on his hands and knees planting young cabbages, but he jumped up and ran after Peter, waving a rake and calling out, "Stop, thief!"

Peter was most dreadfully frightened; he rushed all over the garden, for he had forgotten the way back to the gate. He lost one of his shoes among the cabbages, and the other shoe amongst the potatoes.

     LumosLearning.com

After losing them, he ran on four legs and went faster, so that I think he might have got away altogether if he had not unfortunately run into a gooseberry net, and got caught by the large buttons on his jacket. It was a blue jacket with brass buttons, quite new.

Peter gave himself up for lost, and shed big tears; but his sobs were overheard by some friendly sparrows who flew to him in great excitement, and implored him to exert himself.
Mr. McGregor came up with a sieve, which he intended to pop upon the top of Peter, but Peter wriggled out just in time, leaving his jacket behind him and rushed into the tool-shed, and jumped into a can. It would have been a beautiful thing to hide in if it had not had so much water in it.

Mr. McGregor was quite sure that Peter was somewhere in the tool-shed, perhaps hidden underneath a flower-pot. He began to turn them over carefully, looking under each.

Presently Peter sneezed—"Kerty-schoo!" Mr. McGregor was after him in no time and tried to put his foot upon Peter, who jumped out of a window, upsetting three plants. The window was too small for Mr. McGregor, and he was tired of running after Peter. He went back to his work.

Peter sat down to rest; he was out of breath and trembling with fright, and he had not the least idea which way to go. Also he was very damp with sitting in that can.

After a time he began to wander about, going lippity-lippity—not very fast, and looking all around.

He found a door in a wall but it was locked and there was no room for a fat little rabbit to squeeze underneath.

An old mouse was running in and out over the stone doorstep, carrying peas and beans to her family in the wood. Peter asked her the way to the gate, but she had such a large pea in her mouth that she could not answer. She only shook her head at him. Peter began to cry.

Then he tried to find his way straight across the garden, but he became more and more puzzled. He came to a pond where Mr. McGregor filled his water-cans. A white cat was staring at some goldfish; she sat very, very still; now and then the tip of her tail twitched as if it were alive. Peter thought it best to go away without speaking to her; he had heard about cats from his cousin, little Benjamin Bunny.

He went back toward the tool-shed but suddenly, quite close to him, he heard the noise of a hoe—scr-r-ritch, scratch, scratch, scratch. Peter scurried underneath the bushes. But presently, as nothing happened, he came out, and climbed upon a wheelbarrow, and peeped over. The first thing he saw was Mr. McGregor hoeing onions. His back was turned toward Peter, and beyond him was the gate!

Peter got down very quietly off the wheelbarrow, and started running as fast as he could go, along a straight walk behind some blackcurrant bushes.

Mr. McGregor caught sight of him at the corner, but Peter did not care. He slipped underneath the gate, and was safe at last in the wood outside the garden.

Mr. McGregor hung up the little jacket and the shoes for a scarecrow to frighten the blackbirds.

Peter never stopped running or looked behind him till he got home to the big fir-tree.

He was so tired that he flopped down upon the nice soft sand on the floor of the rabbit-hole, and shut his eyes.

His mother was busy cooking; she wondered what he had done with his clothes. It was the second little jacket and pair of shoes that Peter had lost in a fortnight!

I am sorry to say that Peter was not very well during the evening.

His mother put him to bed, and made some chamomile tea; and she gave a dose of it to Peter!

"One table-spoonful to be taken at bed-time."

But Flopsy, Mopsy, and Cottontail had bread and milk and blackberries for supper. Peter was too tired to even feel he was missing out.

     LumosLearning.com

19. Which was NOT one of the ways Peter Rabbit escaped?

Ⓐ sparrows grabbed him
Ⓑ he jumped out of a window
Ⓒ he swam across a lake
Ⓓ he ran towards the gate

Language Skills

20. Choose the correctly written sentence.

Ⓐ Today is Friday, july 6, 2012.
Ⓑ When are you going two come over to my house.
Ⓒ i will be unable to come to your party.
Ⓓ I am very excited about my birthday on August 8th.

21. Mario is usually a very careful student, but last week he did not study for his spelling test. His teacher wrote on his paper that he was not being careful. What else could the teacher have written?

Ⓐ Mario is caring.
Ⓑ Mario is being careless.
Ⓒ Mario is a careful student.
Ⓓ Mario is always practicing carefulness.

22. Tommy often uses "slang" when talking to his friends. One of his favorite phrases is: "I ain't gonna do it."

He is giving a speech in front of his Boy Scout troop tomorrow evening.

Which of the following could replace Tommy's phrase?

Ⓐ I am not gonna do it.
Ⓑ I ain't going to do it.
Ⓒ I am not going to do it.
Ⓓ I am gonna do it.

23. Read the following sentence.

Choose the answer choice that shows it written entirely CORRECT.

My mom thinks that costs to much money but I disagree

Ⓐ My mom thinks that costs two much money, but I disagree.
Ⓑ My mom thinks that costs too much money but i disagree
Ⓒ My mom thinks that costs too much money, but I disagree.
Ⓓ My Mom thinks that costs too much money, but I disagree.

24. Read the following sentence.

Choose the answer choice that BEST completes the sentence.

I do not want apples _____ oranges with my sandwich.

Ⓐ and
Ⓑ but
Ⓒ or
Ⓓ like

End Of Practice Test 2

          LumosLearning.com

Sample Answer for Writing Task 1

A 5-point response should include:

- Answers to all parts of the question
- Reference to the text in the response
- Personal comparisons

It was the Friday morning that all the third grade students at Cooper's elementary school in New Jersey were waiting for. It was the day when all the third graders would be going to the zoo in Philadelphia. They would be traveling in coach buses for the first time. The bus would have a bathroom and one T.V. for each seat. Everyone was very excited. The most excited person of all was Tim. He was one of the third graders in Mr. Miller's class and for the first time ever was traveling in a coach bus with his mother as a chaperone. She was a little concerned about what could happen when her son goes out of the state without her, so she decided that she would tag along with all of the students. Tim was pleased to see that she was picked to be his chaperone and he was also put with his best friend. Mr. Miller decided that each mother or father would be placed with 5 kids.

Finally, the buses were loaded and everyone was seated with a partner. Each bus could hold 60 people. The bathroom wasn't used much even though it was a long ride to Philadelphia. When all the buses reached the zoo, the students got off in an orderly manner and waited for their teachers and group members.

Tim's mom said to her group, "My name is Mrs. Johnson; if you find saying that isn't simple you may call me Mrs. J. Today is a very special day for all of you. Your Principal, Mr. Albert, has left me in charge of how all of you are going to behave today. If you don't listen to me I will have to write a report to your teacher." She gave them some more instructions and her group was ready to go.

After more instructions from the principal and the chaperones, everyone was ready to go in the zoo. As soon as they went in it started to rain and everyone had to wait inside the lounge. Finally it stopped after a few minutes and everyone was ready to see a zoo. The tour guide came and apologized for the delays. His name was Jack. After a very long time of talking over the zoo rules, the students started walking into a wide hall that was filled with many fish, sort of like an aquarium. After Jack explained about the different kinds of fish that were in the aquarium, he allowed each one of the students in Tim's group to ask three questions. Then the group moved on to see the reptiles such as lizards and many different snakes that made some of the girls scream. They even saw a huge crocodile. It was time for lunch and Jack guided the group to the lunch room and he left. The lunch period was thirty minutes long so everyone had enough time to eat and talk about the interesting exhibits. Then Jack came inside and asked if Tim's group was ready to begin the tour again. Mrs. J and the kids said Yes. excitedly.

Next everyone visited the mammal section of the zoo. Most of the animals were outside. There were gorillas, different kinds of monkeys, tigers, zebras, lions, giraffes, elephants, whales, dolphins, panthers, cheetahs, bears and also polar bears. After about half an hour of explaining all the real and natural habitats of these magnificent animals, Jack decided to take the group to the other side of the mammal exhibit so that they could actually see all of the cool animals. After a few minutes of answering questions they all moved on to the other hallway and out of one of the fancy exit doors. Then they saw all the amazing animals that Jack had talked about. They all started to chatter when they saw the bear roaring and some of the students in Mrs. Carrie's class backed away.

After seeing the birds, the tropical exhibits and many more exhibits, they all said, "Thank you" to Jack, the wonderful guide, and waved goodbye. When everyone finished they came outside and were ready to get back into the bus. It was time to go back to school. Then Mrs. J started the movie and everyone was quiet once again. Everyone had a wonderful day; even if they didn't say it, their faces showed it.

Related Lumos Online Workbook: Let's Talk! (CCSS: W.3.3)

Reading Task 1 Answer Key

Question No.	Answer	Related Lumos Online Workbook	CCSS
1	C	The Question Session	RL.3.1
2	A	The Question Session	RL.3.1
3	C	Tell Me Again... ; Caring Characters and Life's Lessons	RL.3.2
4	B	Calling All Characters ; A Chain of Events	RL.3.3
5	C	Calling All Characters ; A Chain of Events	RL.3.3
6	A	Calling All Characters ; A Chain of Events	RL.3.3

Sample Answer for Open – Ended Question 1

A 4-point response should include:

- Answers to all parts of the question
- References to the text in the response
- Personal comparisons

Hans was a boy who followed whatever directions he was told. He was very well mannered. However, his reaction to his mother's advice was wrong. He did not think before he reacted. If I were Hans, I would not have taken his mother's advice in the same way. I would have thought about the advice his mother was giving and done what was correct. For each present that Grethel gave Hans, he took his mother's advice but in the wrong way. Instead of doing what made sense, he did exactly what his mother said to do and did not think about what he was doing. For example, when Hans' mother told him to put the bacon on his head, he put the calf on his head instead. If I were Hans, I would have thought about what to do with the calf and what would make sense to me. Hans did not really think about what he was doing at all.

Related Lumos Online Workbook: Whose Talking Now? (CCSS: RL.3.6)

     LumosLearning.com

Sample Answer for Writing Task 2

A 5-point response should include:

- Answers to all parts of the question
- References to the text in the response
- Personal comparisons

In this poem, every different creature feels differently about the world. The frog, fly, moth, fern, and lark think the world is a different color and they do not agree on the color the world should be. The only creature that thinks the world is all different colors is the lark.

I agree with the lark because I feel that the world is made up of many different kinds of people. We are all different and special in our own way. People look, act, and feel differently and this is what makes us all so special. This is what I think the lark is trying to teach the other creatures in the poem and is the reason why I agree with his opinion the most.

Related Lumos Online Workbook: Whose Talking Now? (CCSS: RL.3.6)

Reading Task 2 Answer Key

Question No.	Answer	Related Lumos Online Workbook	CCSS
8	B	The Main Idea Arena	RI.3.2
9	B	The Question Session	RI.3.1
10	A	The Main Idea Arena	RI.3.2
11	C	Educational Expressions	RI.3.4
12	A	The Question Session	RI.3.1
13	B	Cause and Effect	RI.3.3

Sample Answer for Open - Ended Question 2

A 4-point response should include:

- Answers to all parts of the question
- References to the text in the response
- Personal comparisons

There are many interesting facts about the Red-Eyed Tree Frog. The Red-Eyed Tree Frog can change its color! The adult frog can be orange, yellow, blue, or reddish-brown. It changes its color depending on how it feels. Another interesting fact about the Red-Eyed Tree Frog is that it has special suction cups on its toes to help it stick to leaves. The suction cups keep the frog from falling off of trees and help it climb better.

Red-Eyed Tree Frogs have bright red eyes that help in escaping from their predators because they scare animals easily. They blend with their surroundings because of their greenish skin color. They are almost invisible when they sleep, which makes it difficult to attack them.

Related Lumos Online Workbook: The Question Session (CCSS: RI.3.1)

Reading Task 3 Answer Key

Question No.	Answer	Related Lumos Online Workbook	CCSS
15	C	The Question Session	RI.3.1
16	B	Educational Expressions	RI.3.4
17	A	The Question Session	RI.3.1

Sample Answer for Open - Ended Question 3

A 4-point response should include:

- Answers to all parts of the question
- References to the text in the response
- Personal comparisons

Albert Einstein was born on March 14, 1879 in Ulm, Germany. His childhood was unusual as he did not speak until he was two and a half years old. He played by himself most of the time as he did not know what he should do with other children. At the age of six he learned to play the violin.

I think Albert Einstein is a genius. At a very young age he was hired as a technical expert at the patent office. While he was working, Einstein developed his own ideas secretly. In 1905 he developed the Theory of Relativity from which he developed a world famous formula which describes the relationship between mass and energy. This theory also provided the new idea about gravity. Einstein received a Nobel prize for his incredible work in physics which shows that he is a genius.

Related Lumos Online Workbook: What Did You Already Know? (CCSS: RI.3.6)

 LumosLearning.com

Reading Task 4 Answer Key

Question No.	Answer	Related Lumos Online Workbook	CCSS
19	C	Calling All Characters	RL.3.3

Language Skills Answer Key

Question No.	Answer	Related Lumos Online Workbook	CCSS
20	D	People, Places and Things ; Replace Those Nouns ; Show Me the Action! ; Tell Me More! ; Make It Make Sense ; Mix Up Those Sentences	L.3.1
21	B	The Context Clue Crew ; Same Name, Different Game ; The Roots and Affix Institute	L.3.4
22	C	Connect the Word for An Effect	L.3.3
23	C	People, Places and Things ; Replace Those Nouns ; Show Me the Action! ; Tell Me More! ; Make It Make Sense ; Mix Up Those Sentences	L.3.1
24	C	People, Places and Things ; Replace Those Nouns ; Show Me the Action! ; Tell Me More! ; Make It Make Sense ; Mix Up Those Sentences	L.3.1

Notes

LumosLearning.com

About Online Workbooks

- When you buy this book, 1 year access to online workbooks included

- Access them anytime from a computer with an internet connection

- Adheres to the New Common Core State Standards

- Includes progress reports

- Instant feedback and self-paced

- Ability to review incorrect answers

- Parents and Teachers can assist in student's learning by reviewing their areas of difficulty

Course Name: NJ ASK Grade 4 Math Prep

Lesson Name:	Correct	Total	% Score	Incorrect
Introduction				
Diagnostic Test		3	0%	3
Number and Numerical Operations				
Workbook - Number Sense	2	10	20%	8
Workbook - Numerical Operations	2	25	8%	23
Workbook - Estimation	1	3	33%	2
Geometry and measurement				
Workbook - Geometric Properties		6	0%	6
Workbook - Transforming Shapes				
Workbook - Coordinate Geometry	1	3	33%	2
Workbook - Units of Measurement				
Workbook - Measuring Geometric Objects	3	10	30%	7
Patterns and algebra				
Workbook - Patterns	7	10	70%	3
Workbook - Functions and relationships				

LESSON NAME: Workbook - Geometric Properties
Elapsed Time: 01.19

Question No. 2
What type of motion is being modeled here?

Select right answer
- ☐ a translation
- ☐ a rotation 90° clockwise
- ☉ a rotation 90° counter-clockwise
- ☐ a reflection

[Previous question] [Next question]

Report Name: Missed Questions

Student Name: Lisa Colbright
Cours Name: NJ ASK Grade 4 Math Prep
Lesson Name: Diagnostic Test

The faces on a number cube are labeled with the numbers 1 through 6. What is the probability of rolling a number greater than 4?

Answer Explanation

(C) On a standard number cube, there are six possible outcomes. Of those outcomes, 2 of them are greater than 4. Thus, the probability of rolling a number greater than 4 is "2 out of 6" or 2/6.

A)		1/6
B)		1/3
C)	Correct Answer	2/6
D)		3/6

Made in the USA
Lexington, KY
17 March 2014